D'Nealian®
Handwriting
Manuscript

Student Edition

1

SAVVAS
LEARNING COMPANY

Acknowledgments

9TL: Bmaki/Shutterstock; 9TC: Urmosi Levente/Shutterstock; 9TR: Irina Rogova/Shutterstock; 9C: Swapan Photography/Shutterstock; 9BC: Holiday.Photo.Top/Shutterstock; 9B: Love the wind/Shutterstock; 10T: Susan Schmitz/Shutterstock; 10TC: HomeStudio/Shutterstock; 10C: Flauma/Shutterstock; 10BL: Tiger Images/Shutterstock; 10BC: BooHoo/Shutterstock; 10BR: Quang Ho/Shutterstock; 24T: Fotogrin/Shutterstock; 24TC: Mekdes.k/Shutterstock; 24C: Neil Lang/Shutterstock; 24BC: Nagel Photography/Shutterstock; 24B: Bogdanovich_Alexander/Shutterstock; 40: Studiovin/Shutterstock; 48L: Potapov Alexander/Shutterstock; 48R: LightField Studios/Shutterstock; 49TL: Michael Jay Berlin/Shutterstock; 49TC: Africa Studio/Shutterstock; 49TR: Montego/Shutterstock; 49CL: Nynke Van Holten/Shutterstock; 49C: LoopAll/Shutterstock; 49CR: Pixel-Shot/Shutterstock; 49BL: Paleka/Shutterstock; 49BC: Yulia Yudaeva/Shutterstock; 49BR: Nathapol Kongseang/Shutterstock; 50: Studiovin/Shutterstock; 55L: Alex Zaitsev/Shutterstock; 55R: Olga Alyonkina/Shutterstock; 61L: Tania Zbrodko/Shutterstock; 61R: Irina Nartova/Shutterstock; 62: Studiovin/Shutterstock; 68: Lu Yago/Shutterstock; 70: Studiovin/Shutterstock; 74: Studiovin/Shutterstock; 78T: Jiang Hongyan/Shutterstock; 78C: Hong Vo/Shutterstock; 78B: Nataly Studio/Shutterstock; 79T: Andrey Eremin/Shutterstock; 79C: Bergamont/Shutterstock; 79B: BW Folsom/Shutterstock; 80T: Hong Vo/Shutterstock; 80C: Arigato/Shutterstock; 80B: Maliflower73/Shutterstock; 81T: Sakarin Sawasdinaka/Shutterstock; 81C: Rodrigobark/Shutterstock; 81B: Bergamont/Shutterstock; 82: Studiovin/Shutterstock; 83: Mindscape studio/Shutterstock; 84: Hryshchyshen Serhii/Shutterstock; 90T: FoxyImage/Shutterstock; 90B: FoxyImage/Shutterstock; 92: Ondrej Prosicky/Shutterstock; 108: Studiovin/Shutterstock; 118: Studiovin/Shutterstock; 128: Studiovin/Shutterstock; 130: Stockphoto Mania/Shutterstock; 135: Krytaeva Iana/Shutterstock; 136TL: Vaclav Volrab/Shutterstock; 136TR: Marina Zezelina/Shutterstock; 136BL: Rusya007/Shutterstock; 136BR: Smileus/Shutterstock; 137T: Anchalee Ar/Shutterstock; 137B: FoxyImage/Shutterstock; 139: Solmariart/Shutterstock

ISBN-13: 978-1-4183-6172-3

ISBN-10: 1-4183-6172-0

SAVVAS
LEARNING COMPANY

Table of Contents

Unit One

Getting Ready to Write

Sitting Position for Writing

Sit tall.
Put both feet on the floor.

Left-handed

Right-handed

Students position themselves comfortably for writing.

Right-handed Position for Writing

Slant your paper as shown in the picture.

Hold it with your left hand.

Hold your pencil lightly between your fingers.

Study the picture.

Students practice the proper position of their papers and pencils for good writing.

Left-handed Position for Writing

Slant your paper as shown in the picture.

Hold it with your right hand.

Hold your pencil lightly between your fingers.

Study the picture.

Students practice the proper position of their papers and pencils for good writing.

Circle the pictures.

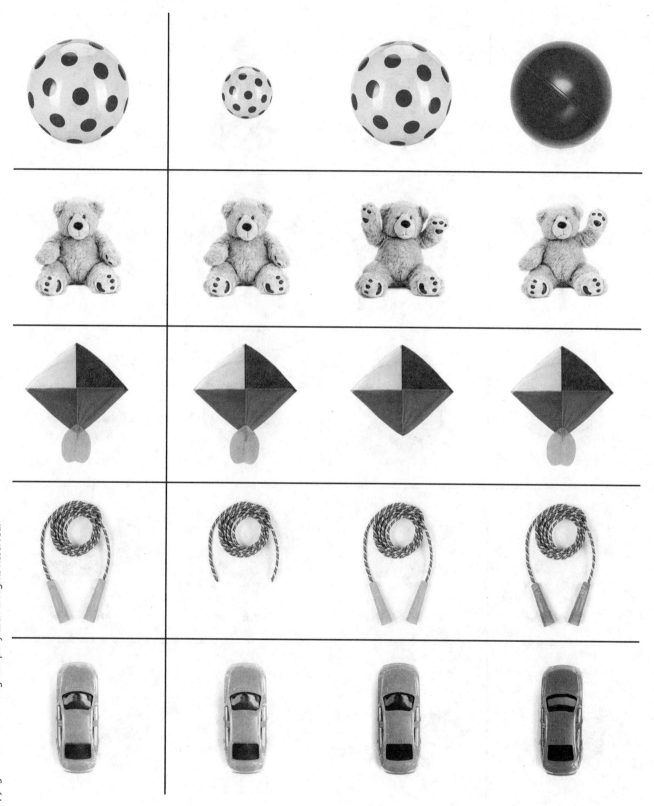

Students circle the picture that matches the first one in each row.

Circle the pictures.

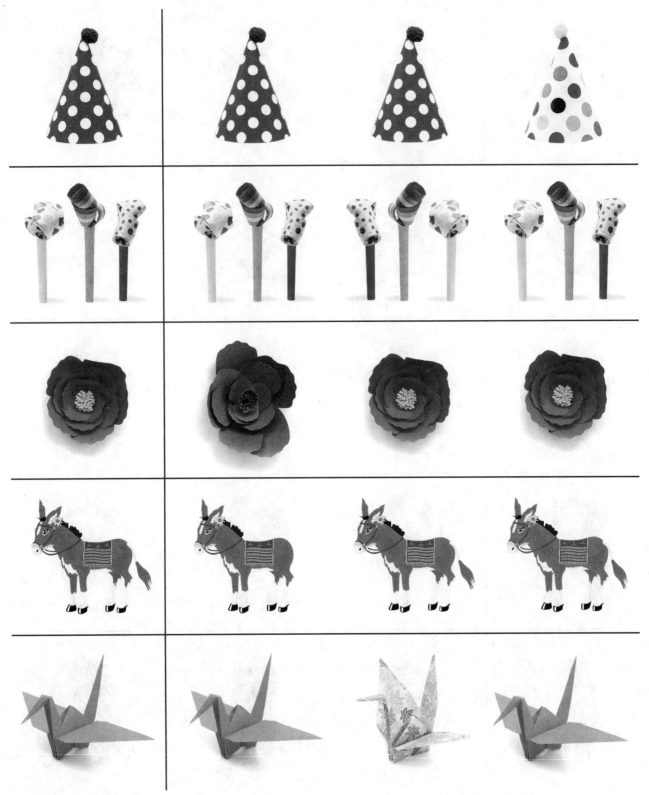

Students circle the picture that is different in each row.

Draw and color.

Students draw a window with blue curtains on the **top** floor, a window with yellow curtains on the **middle** floor, and a window with green curtains on the **bottom** floor.

Draw and color.

12 Prewriting: Spatial Relationships

Students draw the footpath **around** the art fair.

Mark the pictures.

Prewriting: Spatial Relationships **13**

Students circle each animal **above** the water.
and underline each animal **below** the water.

Mark the pictures.

14 Prewriting: Spatial Relationships

Students circle each puppet **over** the table and underline each child **under** the table.

Draw the lines.

Prewriting: Eye-Hand Coordination **15**

Students locate the arrows and the starting dots. Then they draw lines within the paths to the dots at the end.

Draw a line.

16 Prewriting: Eye-Hand Coordination

Students locate the arrow and the starting dot. Then
they draw a line within the path to the dot at the end.

Trace the tools.
Color.

Prewriting: Fine-Motor Coordination   **17**

Students trace and color the tools for the garden.

Trace and color.
Cut and paste.

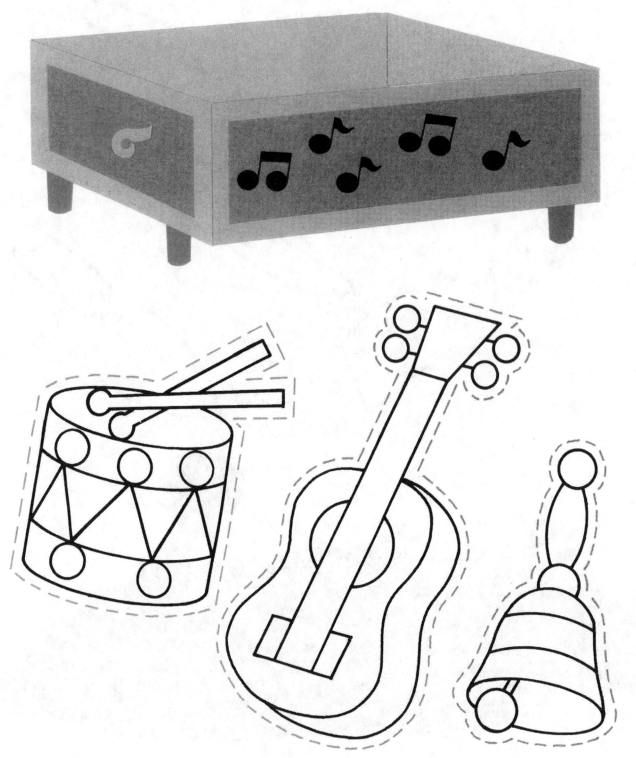

18 Prewriting: Fine-Motor Coordination

Students color and trace the instruments at the bottom of the page.
Then they cut out the instruments and paste them in the music chest.

Draw the lines.

Prewriting: Left-to-Right Progression **19**

Students locate the arrows and the starting dots. Then they draw lines within the paths to the dots at the end.

Draw the lines.

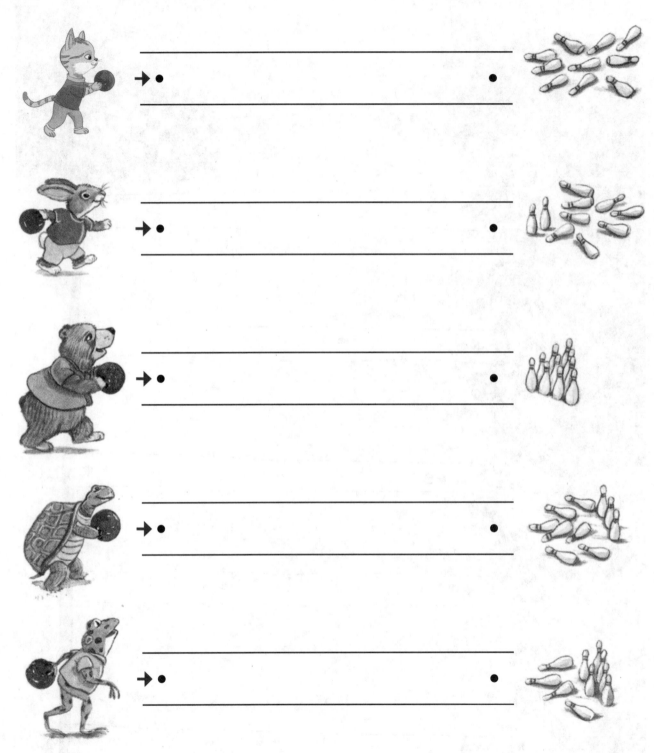

Prewriting: Left-to-Right Progression

Students locate the arrows and the starting dots. Then
they draw lines within the paths to the dots at the end.

Match.
Circle the letters.

a | l r o a

y | n u y c

h | h m t w

p | q p b g

j | i j k d

Students circle the letter that matches the first one in each row.

Match.
Circle the letters.

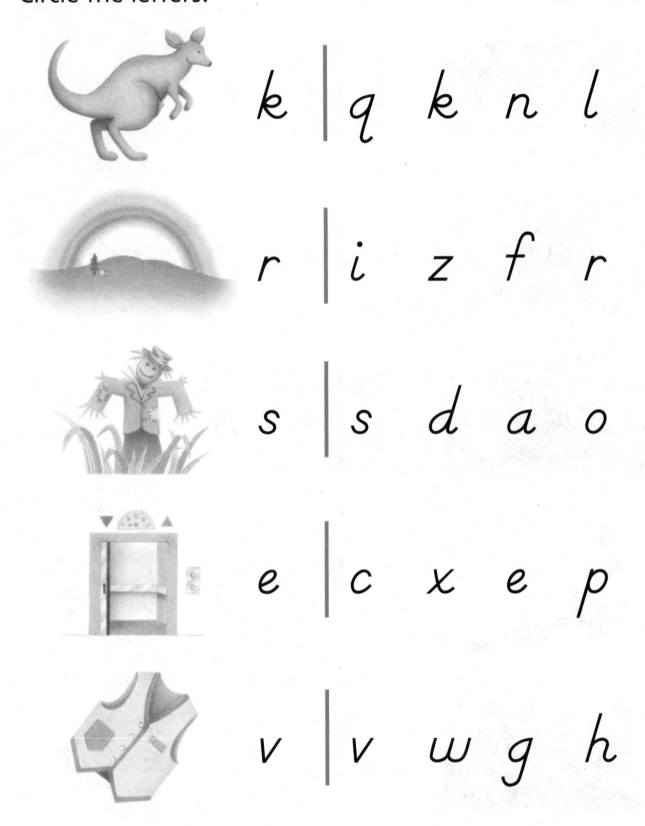

k | q k n l

r | i z f r

s | s d a o

e | c x e p

v | v w g h

22 Prewriting: Letter Discrimination

Students circle the letter that matches the first one in each row.

Match.
Circle the letters.

I | T I J K

B | A Z B P

D | D R O S

C | Q V C Y

W | E U M W

Students circle the letter that matches the first one in each row.

Match.
Circle the letters.

T	L	N	T	E
M	M	I	J	P
O	D	O	U	B
G	W	G	C	X
Z	H	R	A	Z

24 Prewriting: Letter Discrimination

Students circle the letter that matches the first one in each row.

Draw and color.

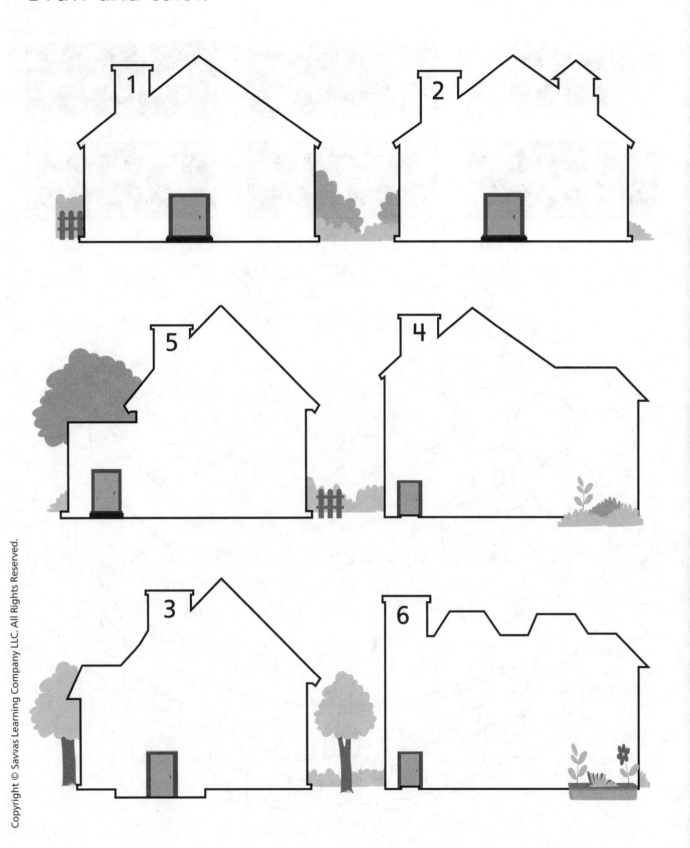

Students draw and color a specific number of windows in each picture to represent the number shown.

Match and color.

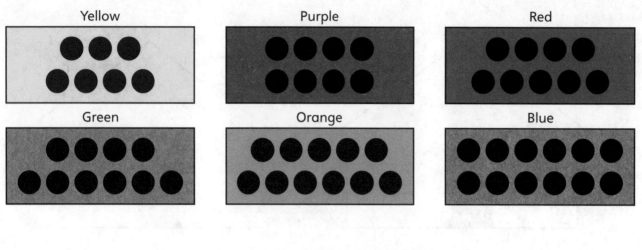

Yellow

Purple

Red

Green

Orange

Blue

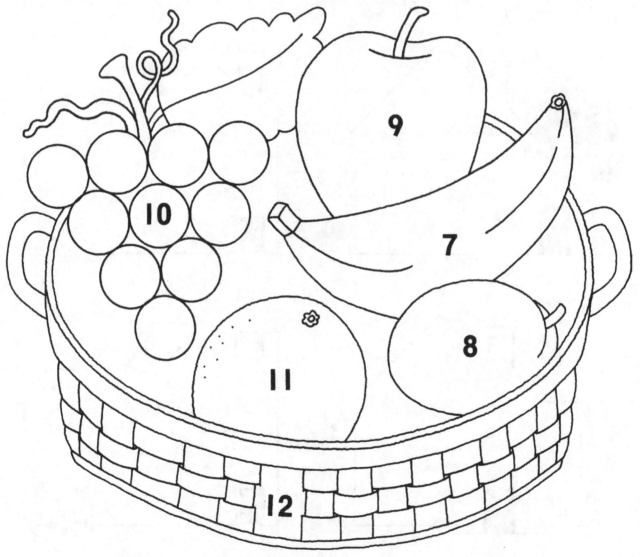

26 Prewriting: Number Discrimination

Students match the number of dots in each box with
the matching number on the fruit and color the picture.

Animals can help you remember the size of letters.

 A is tall.

These letters are tall.

b d f h k l t

 An is small.

These letters are small.

a c e i m n o

r s u v w x z

 A has a tail that falls.

These letters fall.

g j p q y

Students compare the size of animals
to the relative size of lowercase letters.

Look at the size of each letter.
Draw the correct animal to match each group.

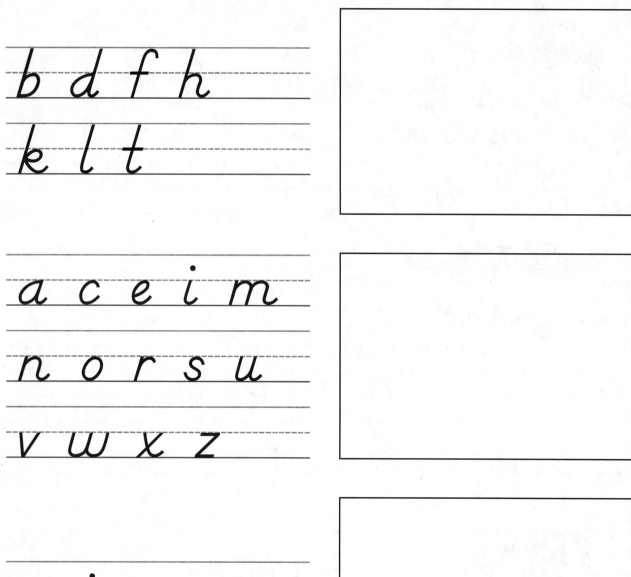

b d f h

k l t

a c e i m

n o r s u

v w x z

g j p q y

Students draw a picture of a giraffe to represent tall letters, an alligator
to represent small letters, and a tiger to represent descender letters.

Letters should slant the same way.
Color the kites that can fly.

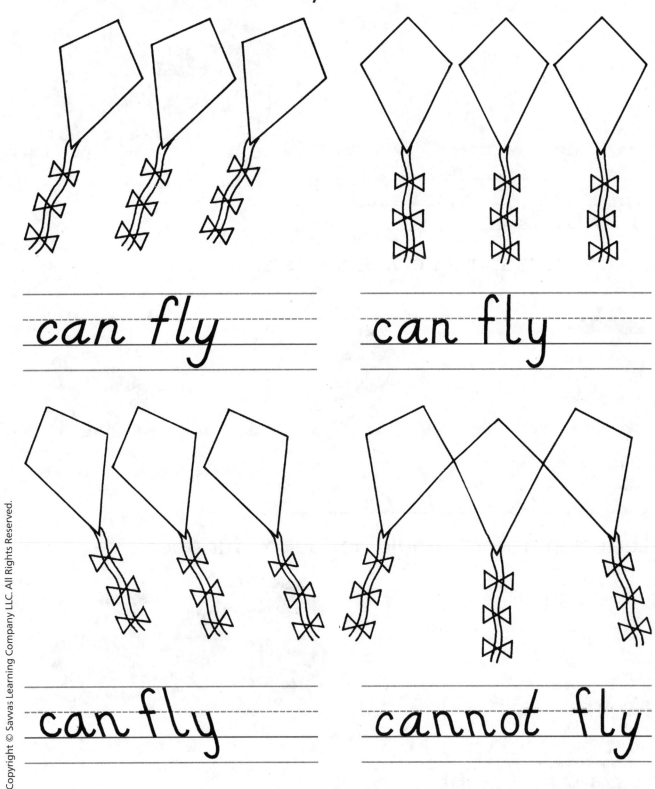

can fly

can fly

can fly

cannot fly

Students compare the slant of each group of kites to the letters in each group.
Then they color each group of kites that is slanted in the same direction.

You need to space letters and words.
Letters in a word should not be too close.

too close

Leave more space between letters.

t o o   f a r

Letters in a word should not be too far apart.

just fine

Students compare correct and incorrect letter and word spacing.

Unit Two

Writing Lowercase Letters

There are many ways to write the same letter.
Circle each **p**.
Draw a line under each **o**.
Draw a box around each **e**.

Home
Sweet
Home

popcorn

noodles

rice

sponge

HOT **COLD**

Soap

towels

Students compare the same letters in different type styles. Then they
circle each **p**, underline each **o**, and draw a box around each **e**.

apple

ant

$\bar{a}$

$\bar{a}$ a a a

a

a

My Words

Writing **a**   **33**

Students trace and write the letter **a** and the word **a**.

d

dog

d d d · · d

add

add

dad

dad

My Words

34 Writing **d**

Students trace and write the letter **d** and the words **add** and **dad**.

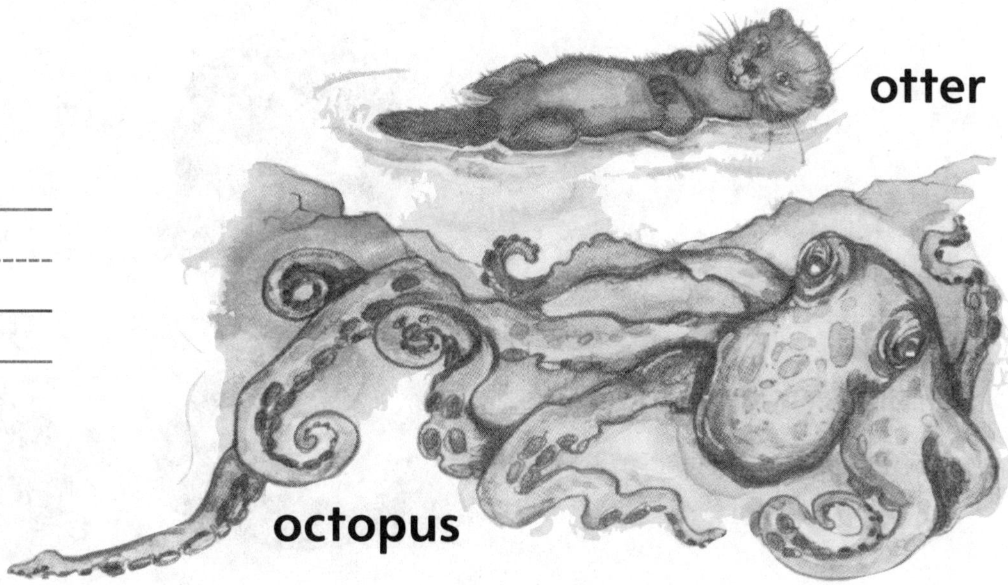

otter

Ō

octopus

Ō   O   O   •   •   O

odd

odd

My Words

Students trace and write the letter **o** and the word **odd**.

girl

gift

g

g   g   g   g

dog

dog

good

good

My Words

36 Writing **g**

Students trace and write the letter **g** and the words **dog** and **good**.

cat

coat

C

C   C   C   C

cocoa

cocoa

My Words

Writing **c**   37

Students trace and write the letter **c** and the word **cocoa**.

elephant

eggs

e

e   *e*   *e*   •   •   *e*

•   •   •   •   •   •

•   •   •   •   •   •

•   •   •   •   •   •

egg

egg

My Words

38 Writing **e**

Students trace and write the letter **e** and the word **egg**.

sun

S

sandbox

S   S   S   •   •   S

sea

sea

see

see

My Words

Writing s   39

Students trace and write the letter **s** and the words **sea** and **see**.

Practice

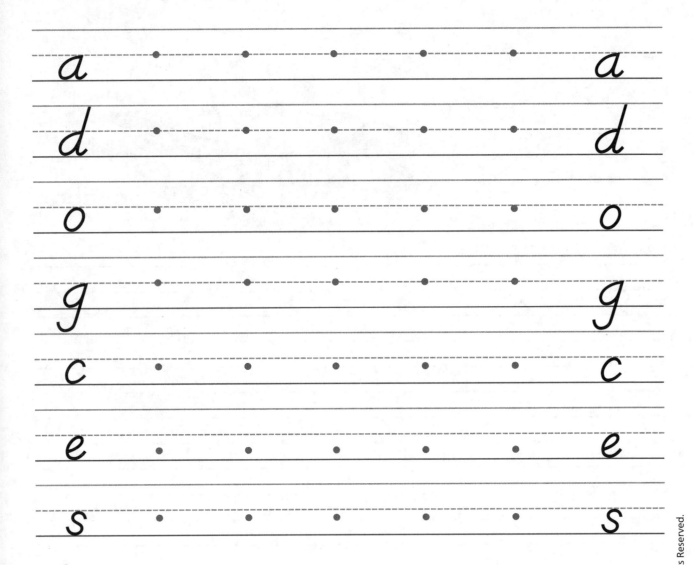

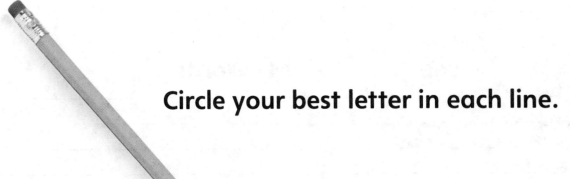

Circle your best letter in each line.

Students write the letters **a**, **d**, **o**, **g**, **c**, **e**, and **s**.

Review

dog

dog

dogs

dogs

cage

cage

cages

cages

goose

goose

geese

geese

seed

seed

seeds

seeds

Review **41**

Students trace and write words with the letters **a**, **d**, **o**, **g**, **c**, **e**, and **s**.

Evaluation

Remember: Close the letters **a**, **d**, **o**, and **g**.

dad

dad

cage

cage

a goose

a goose

good dogs

good dogs

Check Your Handwriting

	Yes	No
Did you close the letters **a**, **d**, **o**, and **g**?	☐	☐

Students trace and write words and phrases
with the letters **a**, **d**, **o**, **g**, **c**, **e**, and **s**.

f

fish

fence

f f f f

off

off

feed

feed

My Words

Writing **f**   **43**

Students trace and write the letter **f** and the words **off** and **feed**.

boy

ball

b b b b b

base

base

bag

bag

My Words

44   Writing **b**

Students trace and write the letter **b** and the words **base** and **bag**.

lion

lake

l

l l l l

leaf

leaf

fall

fall

My Words

Students trace and write the letter **l** and the words **leaf** and **fall**.

tent

telescope

t t t t

late

late

best

best

My Words

Writing **t**

Students trace and write the letter **t** and the words **late** and **best**.

h

hook

hat

ʰh   h   h   h

hat

hat

hall

hall

My Words

Writing **h**   **47**

Students trace and write the letter **h** and the words **hat** and **hall**.

key

kitchen

k

k   *k*   *k*   *k*

bake

bake

cook

cook

My Words

48 Writing **k**

Students trace and write the letter **k** and the words **bake** and **cook**.

Write each word.

tag

_____

- - - - - - - - - - - -

_____

bag

_____

- - - - - - - - - - - -

_____

flag

_____

- - - - - - - - - - - -

_____

goat

_____

- - - - - - - - - - - -

_____

boat

_____

- - - - - - - - - - - -

_____

coat

_____

- - - - - - - - - - - -

_____

sock

_____

- - - - - - - - - - - -

lock

_____

- - - - - - - - - - - -

clock

_____

- - - - - - - - - - - -

Students write words without a handwriting model.

Practice

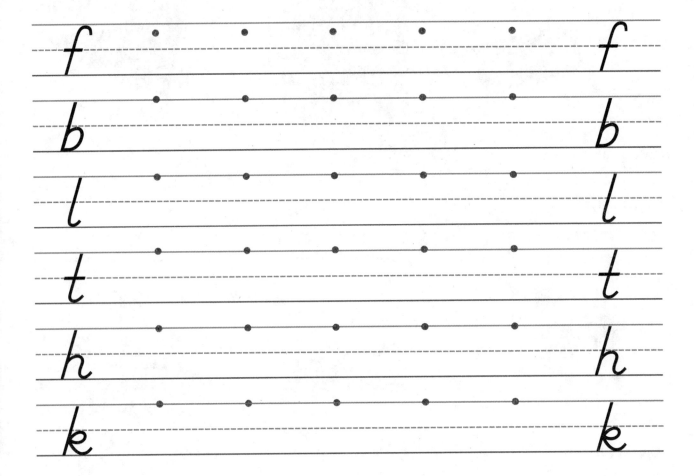

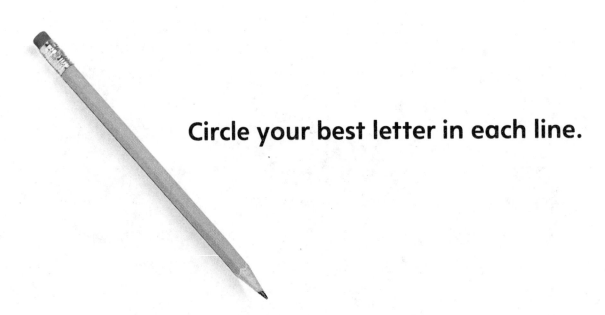

Circle your best letter in each line.

Students write the letters **f**, **b**, **l**, **t**, **h**, and **k**.

Review

basket

basket

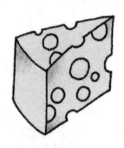
cheese

cheese

bat

bat

ball

ball

flags

flags

badge

badge

socks

socks

hat

hat

Students trace and write words with the letters **f**, **b**, **l**, **t**, **h**, and **k**.

Evaluation

Remember: Cross the letters **f** and **t**.

look

look

hot

hot

fast softball

fast softball

a baseball bat

a baseball bat

Check Your Handwriting

Did you cross the letters **f** and **t**?

Yes ☐   No ☐

Students trace and write words and
phrases with the letters **f, b, l, t, h**, and **k**.

igloo

i

4 —
3 —
2 —
1 —
Inch **inch**

i i i • • i

igloo

igloo

My Words

Students trace and write the letter **i** and the word **igloo**.

umpire

umbrella

u

u u u u

us

bus

My Words

us

bus

54   Writing **u**

Students trace and write the letter **u** and the words **us** and **bus**.

w

wall

web

w   *w*   *w*   *w*

web

web

wall

wall

My Words

Writing w   55

Students trace and write the letter **w** and the words **web** and **wall**.

y

yard

yarn

y   y   y   •   •   y

yellow

yellow

My Words

Students trace and write the letter y and the word **yellow**.

jack-in-the-box

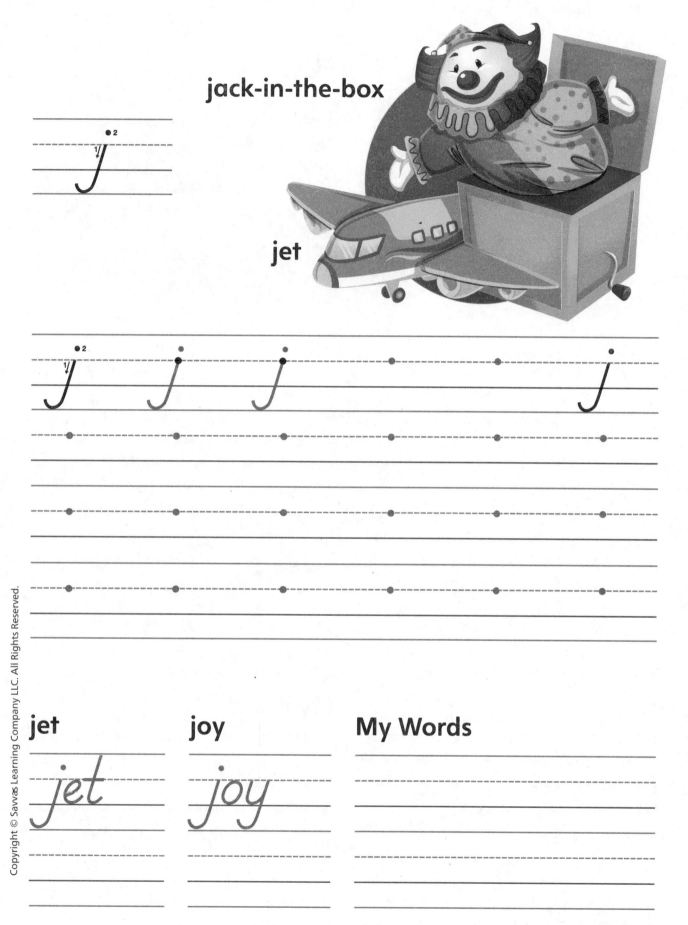

jet

j j j   j

jet

jet

joy

joy

My Words

Students trace and write the letter **j** and the words **jet** and **joy**.

rabbit   **rock**

r

r   *r*   *r*   *r*

rabbit

rabbit

My Words

58   Writing **r**

Students trace and write the letter **r** and the word **rabbit**.

nightingales

nest

n

n   *n*   *n*   *n*

nest   **sing**   **My Words**

nest   *sing*

Students trace and write the letter **n** and the words **nest** and **sing**.

moon

m

mountain

m   m   m   m

moon

moon

My Words

Students trace and write the letter **m** and the word **moon**.

puppet

paper

p

p   p   p   p

puppet

puppet

My Words

Writing **p**   **61**

Students trace and write the letter **p** and the word **puppet**.

Practice

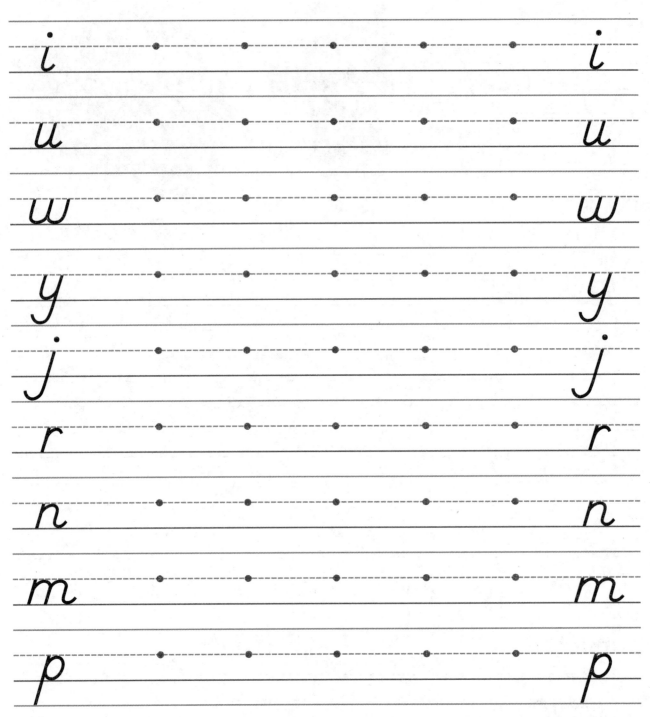

i   i

u   u

w   w

y   y

j   j

r   r

n   n

m   m

p   p

Circle your best letter in each line.

62 Practice

Students write the letters **i**, **u**, **w**, **y**, **j**, **r**, **n**, **m**, and **p**.

Review

cup

cup

jar

jar

bowl

bowl

milk

milk

kitchen

kitchen

strawberry

strawberry

Students trace and write words with the letters **i, u, w, y, j, r, n, m,** and **p.**

Evaluation

Remember: Dot the letters **i** and **j**.

home

home

juice

juice

big party

big party

a few friends

a few friends

Check Your Handwriting

Did you dot the letters **i** and **j**?

	Yes	No
	☐	☐

Students trace and write words and phrases
with the letters **i, u, w, y, j, r, n, m,** and **p**.

q

queen

quarter

q   q   q   q   q

quarter

quarter

My Words

Students trace and write the letter **q** and the word **quarter**.

valentine

V

violets

V V V V · · V

· · · · · ·

· · · · · ·

· · · · · ·

valentine

valentine

My Words

66 Writing **v**

Students trace and write the letter **v** and the word **valentine**.

$\vec{Z}$

zebra

$\vec{Z}$　Z　Z　Z　　　　　　Z

zebra

zebra

My Words

Students trace and write the letter **z** and the word **zebra**.

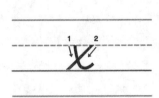

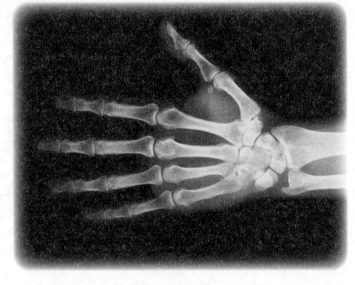

x-ray

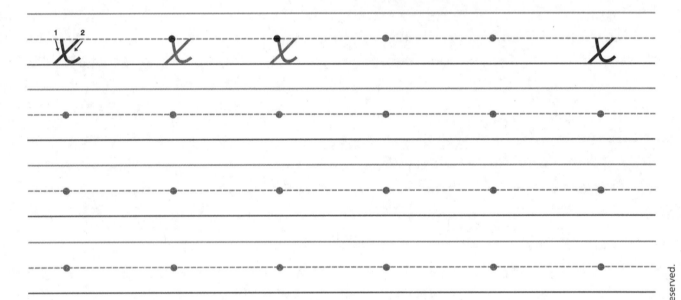

x-ray

x-ray

My Words

68 Writing **x**

Students trace and write the letter **x** and the word **x-ray**.

Each pair of words makes a new word.
Write each new word.

door   **bell**   **doorbell**
_____
_____
_____

mail   **box**   **mailbox**
_____
_____
_____

bird   **house**   **birdhouse**
_____
_____
_____

fish   **net**   **fishnet**
_____
_____
_____

hair   **cut**   **haircut**
_____
_____
_____

Students write words without a handwriting model.

Practice

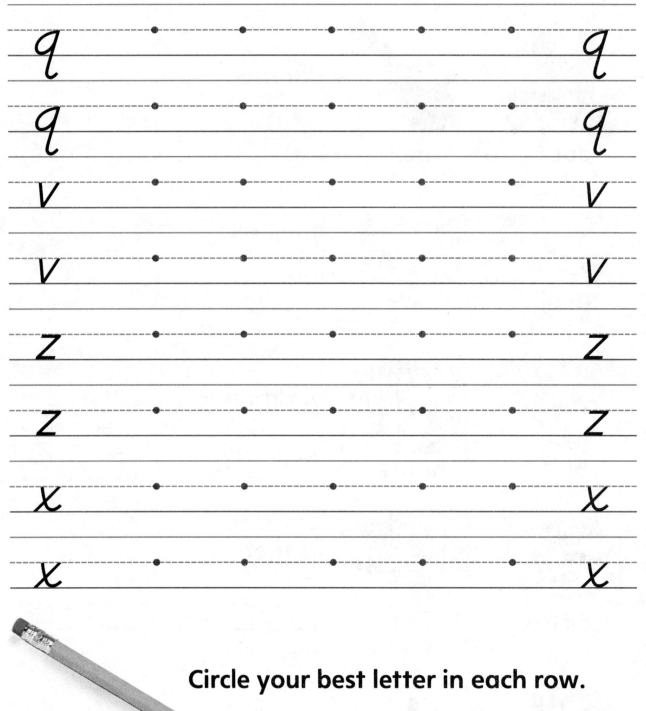

Circle your best letter in each row.

70 Practice

Students write the letters **q**, **v**, **z**, and **x**.

Review

ox

ox

fox

fox

quail

quail

zebra

zebra

beaver

beaver

lizard

lizard

Students trace and write words with the letters **q**, **v**, **z**, and **x**.

Evaluation

Remember: Slant all letters the same way.

zoo

zoo

view

view

six animals

six animals

a quiet bear

a quiet bear

Check Your Handwriting

Do all your letters slant the same way?

Yes ☐   No ☐

Students trace and write words and phrases with the letters **q, v, z**, and **x**.

Writing a Spelling Test

Good handwriting helps you do well on spelling tests.
Good handwriting makes your words easy to read.

Getting Ready

- Write your name neatly on your paper.
- Number your paper.
- Write one number for each word you will spell.

Writing the Words

- Listen to your teacher.
- Be sure you know what word to write.
- Use your best handwriting.
- All your letters should slant the same way.
- Letters should not be too close together or too far apart.

3. Boy

- If you make a mistake, fix it as your teacher tells you.
  Which should you do?
  Draw a line through it and rewrite it. ☐
  Erase it carefully and rewrite it. ☐

Copyright © Savvas Learning Company LLC. All Rights Reserved.

Students learn that good handwriting will help them do well on spelling tests.

Here is a spelling test that Kristen wrote.

Kristen

1. bring

2. job

3. pink

4. ~~kuik~~ quick

5. yet

6. kite

Look at how Kristen wrote her spelling test.　　Yes　No

- Do all her letters slant the same way?
- Is the space between each letter the same?
- Did she fix mistakes carefully?
- Is her handwriting easy to read?

Circle words that do not have the correct slant.

What letters do not have the correct spacing?

Make a line under them.

Now you write Kristen's spelling words.
Write your own name at the top.

Check your handwriting.

Yes No

- Do all your letters slant the same way?
- Is the space between each letter the same?
- Did you fix mistakes carefully?
- Is your handwriting easy to read?

Make any changes that are needed.
Then show how you would correct a mistake.

The a b c's are not hard to do.
Just say the letters and write them too.

a   b   c   d

e   f   g   h

i   j   k   l

m   n   o   p

q   r   s   t

u   v   w

x   y   z

76 Cumulative Review

Students trace and write each lowercase letter of the alphabet.

Unit Three

Writing Numbers and Number Words

Trace and write.

1 1 1   one

one

2 2 2   two

two

3 3 3   three

three

78 Writing **1, 2, 3, one, two, three**

Students trace and write the numbers **1, 2,**
and **3** and the words **one, two,** and **three.**

Trace and write.

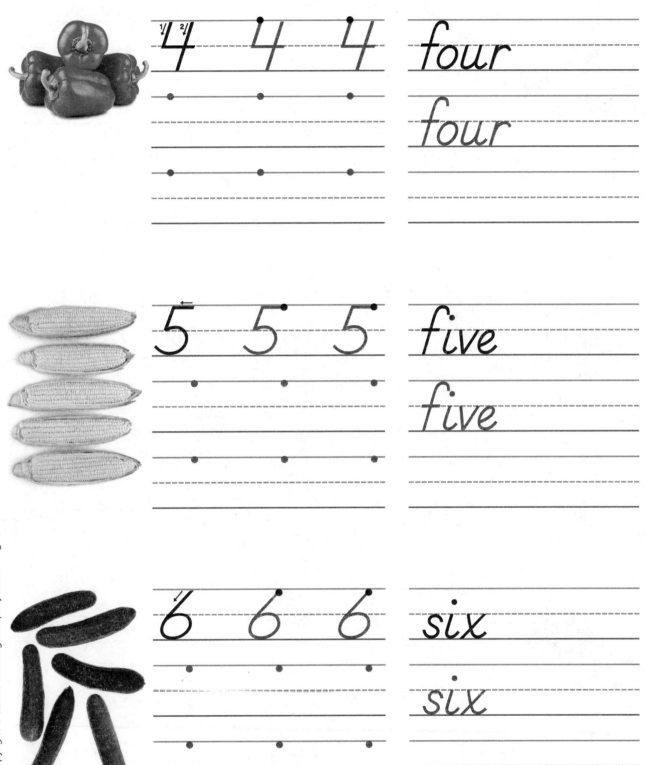

4   4   4   *four*

                                                            four

5   5   5   *five*

  five

6   6   6   *six*

  six

Students trace and write the numbers **4**, **5**, and **6** and the words **four**, **five**, and **six**.

Trace and write.

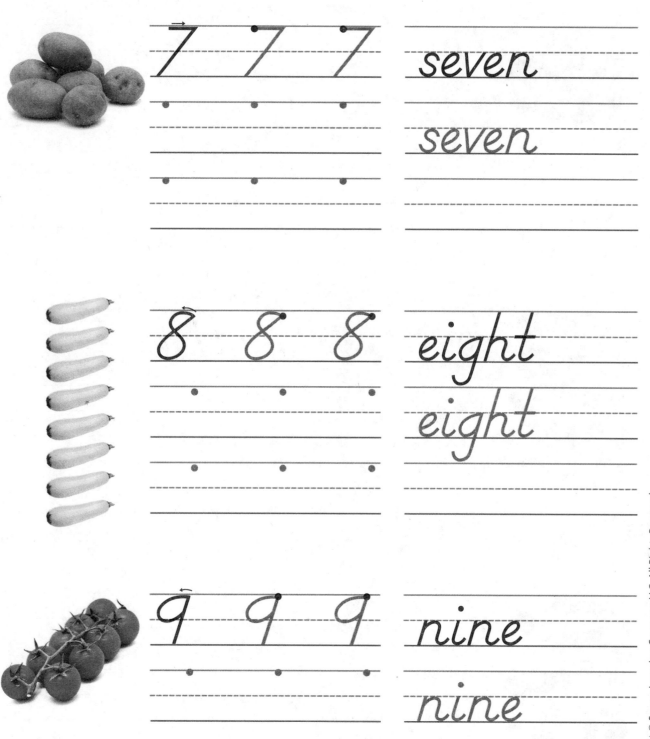

7 7 7   seven

seven

8 8 8   eight

eight

9 9 9   nine

nine

Students trace and write the numbers **7, 8,**
and **9** and the words **seven**, **eight**, and **nine**.

Trace and write.

ten

ten

eleven

eleven

twelve

twelve

Students trace and write the numbers **10**, **11**, and **12** and the words **ten**, **eleven**, and **twelve**.

Practice

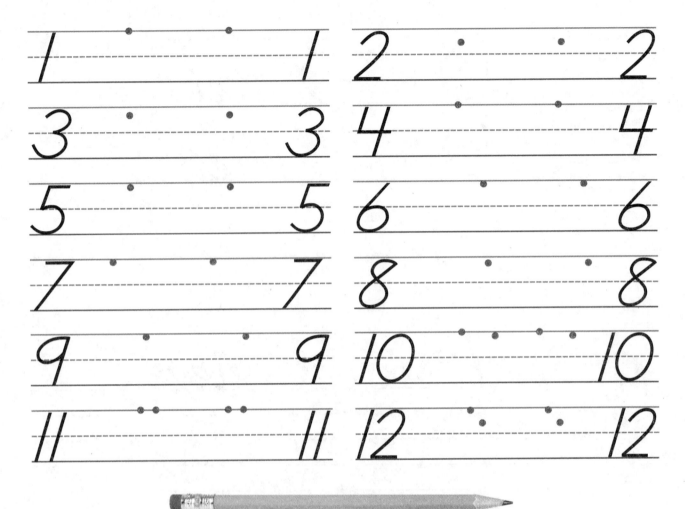

Circle your best number in each line.
Write the numbers **1**, **2**, **3**, **4**, **5**, and **6**.

_____

- -

_____

Write the numbers **7**, **8**, **9**, **10**, **11**, and **12**.

_____

- -

_____

82   Practice

Students write the numbers **1** through **12**.

Review

one	1	two	2
one	*1*	*two*	*2*

three	3	four	4
three	*3*	*four*	*4*

five	5	six	6
five	*5*	*six*	*6*

seven	7	eight	8
seven	*7*	*eight*	*8*

Students trace and write the words **one** through
eight and the numbers **1** through **8**.

Evaluation

Remember: Close the numbers **9** and **0**.

nine   **9**   ten   **10**

nine   *9*   *ten*   *10*

eleven   **11**   twelve   **12**

eleven   *11*   *twelve*   *12*

Check Your Handwriting

Did you close the numbers **9** and **0**?

Yes   No

☐   ☐

84   Evaluation

Students trace and write the words **nine** through
twelve and the numbers **9** through **12**.

Unit Four

Writing Capital Letters

There are many ways to write capital letters.
Circle each **F** and **f**.
Draw a line under each **T** and **t**.
Draw a box around each **S** and **s**.
Now draw a path from the house to the school.

Fine Foods

Trash

U. S. Mail

Bus Stop

Ash Street

Gas for Sale

STOP

Fox School

Students compare the same letters in different type styles. Then they circle each **F** and **f**, underline each **T** and **t**, and draw a box around each **S** and **s**.

Write all the tall letters.

b d f h k l t

All the capital letters are tall letters too.

A B C D E F G H I
J K L M N O P Q R
S T U V W X Y Z

Write all the small letters.

a c e i m n o r s u v w x z

Write all the letters that fall.

g j p q y

Letter Size and Form   **87**

Students write the tall letters, the small letters, and the
descender letters. Then they name the capital letters.

Name all the letters in each group.

Tall Letters

b d f h k l t

A B C D E F G

H I J K L M N

O P Q R S T

U V W X Y Z

Small Letters

a c e i m n o

r s u v w x z

Letters That Fall

g j p q y

Draw a line under the tall letters.
Circle the small letters.
Draw a box around the letters that fall.

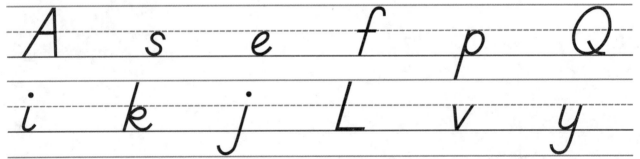

A   s   e   f   p   Q

i   k   j   L   v   y

88 Letter Size and Form

Students distinguish different letter sizes. Then they underline the tall letters,
circle the small letters, and draw a box around the descender letters.

All your letters should slant the same way.
You can slant your letters three ways.

straight up and down

Big Top

to the right

Big Top

to the left

Big Top

Read the words.
Circle the words that have the correct slant.

Circus Town

amazing acrobats

joyful jugglers

Jojo Clown

Students circle the words that show all the
letters slanted in the same direction.

You need to space letters and words.

Do not write letters in a word too close together.

The band cannot play

Do not write letters in a word too far apart.

The band ca

Leave more space between words.

The band can play.

Now write these words.
Ask a friend to read the words.

a marching song

90 Letter and Word Spacing

Students compare correct and incorrect letter and word spacing. Then they write a phrase using correct spacing.

Every letter has a capital and lowercase form.

Aa Bb Cc Dd Ee Ff Gg

Hh Ii Jj Kk Ll Mm

Nn Oo Pp Qq Rr Ss Tt

Uu Vv Ww Xx Yy Zz

Read the riddles. Write the answers.
Use lowercase letters.

What fish shines like a star?
Ss Tt Aa Rr Ff Ii Ss Hh

_____

_____

What fish says meow?
Cc Aa Tt Ff Ii Ss Hh

_____

_____

What fish is very rich?
Gg Oo Ll Dd Ff Ii Ss Hh

_____

_____

Letter Comparison **91**

Students compare capital and lowercase letters of the alphabet.
Then they write responses to riddles using the lowercase alphabet.

Read the rhyme.
Circle these marks.

?	.	'	,

Draw a line under the capital letters.

A Wise Old Owl

A wise old owl lived in an oak,
The more he saw the less he spoke.
The less he spoke the more he heard.
Why can't we all be like that wise old bird?

Trace and write.

? ? ?

Now read the rhyme again.
Put these marks in the correct place.

?	.	'	,

A Wise Old Owl

A wise old owl lived in an oak ☐

The more he saw the less he spoke ☐

The less he spoke the more he heard ☐

Why can ☐ t we all be like that wise old bird ☐

92 Punctuation

Students identify, trace, and write question marks, periods, apostrophes, and commas. Then they write punctuation marks to complete sentences in a rhyme.

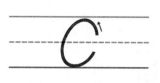

C

Cousin Cora

cup

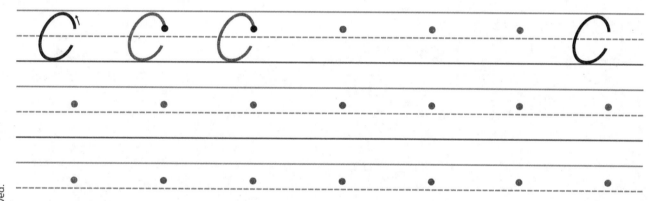

C C C C · · · C

Cora liked the soup.

Cora liked the soup.

Students trace and write the letter **C** and the sentence **Cora liked the soup.**

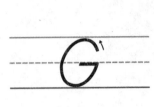

goggles

Gary Goat

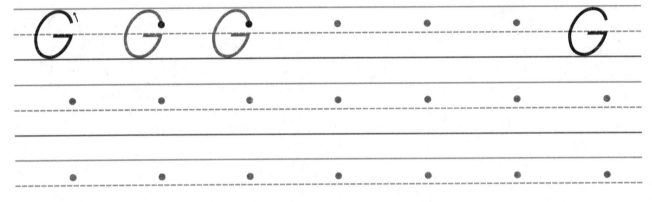

Gary did not feel well.

Gary did not feel well.

Students trace and write the letter **G** and the sentence **Gary did not feel well.**

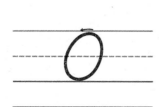

Oscar Ox

ostrich

Oscar was glad to help.

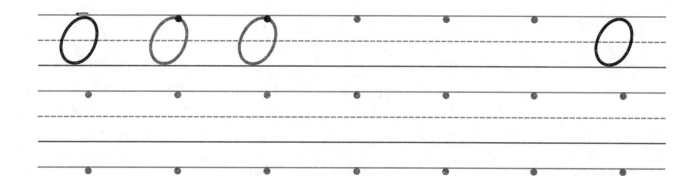

Students trace and write the letter **O** and the sentence **Oscar was glad to help.**

Quint Quade

quilt

Quint has a quilt.

Quint has a quilt.

96 Writing **Q**

Students trace and write the letter **Q** and the sentence **Quint has a quilt.**

S

Sumi Seal

seagulls

S S S · · · S

Sumi sails her boat.

Sumi sails her boat.

Students trace and write the letter **S** and the sentence **Sumi sails her boat.**

Practice

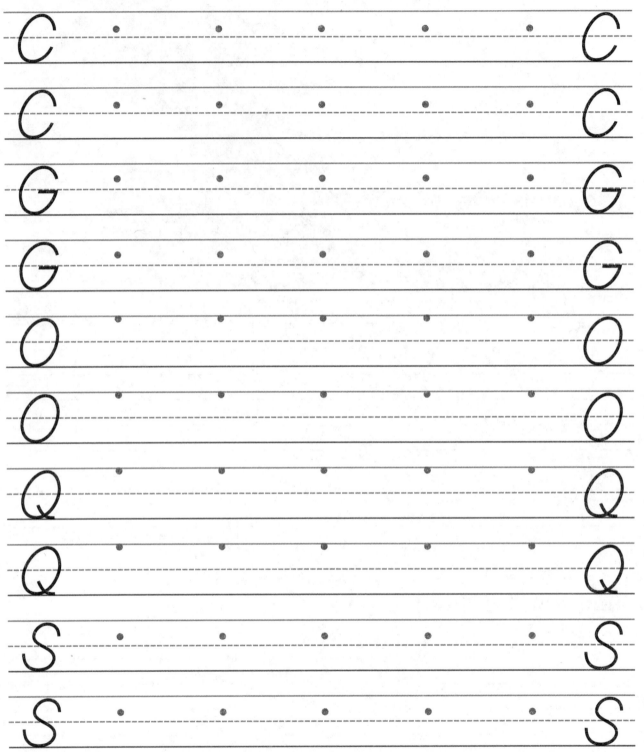

Circle your best letter in each line.

Students write the letters **C, G, O, Q,** and **S.**

Review

Gary

Gary

Oscar

Oscar

Cousin Cora

Cousin Cora

Quint Quade

Quint Quade

Sumi Seal

Sumi Seal

Students trace and write names with the letters **C**, **G**, **O**, **Q**, and **S**.

Evaluation

Remember: Curve the letters **C**, **G**, **O**, and **S**.

Doctor Colt

Doctor Ox

Gabe and Sadie are sick.

Gabe and Sadie are sick.

Can Omar help them?

Can Omar help them?

Check Your Handwriting

Did you curve the letters **C**, **G**, **O**, and **S**?

Yes ☐   No ☐

100   Evaluation

Students trace and write sentences with the letters **C**, **G**, **O**, and **S**.

insect

Isabel Inns

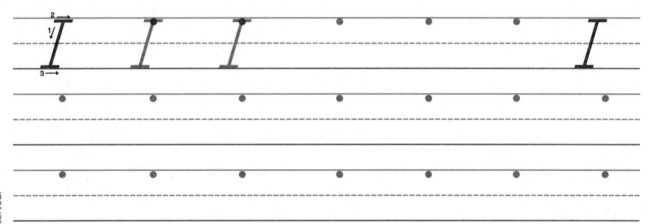

Isabel sees an insect.

Isabel sees an insect.

Writing **I**   **101**

Students trace and write the letter **I** and the sentence **Isabel sees an insect.**

ledges

Lucy Lizard

Lucy crawls slowly.

Lucy crawls slowly.

102 Writing **L**

Students trace and write the letter **L** and the sentence **Lucy crawls slowly.**

telephone

Toni Turtle

T

T   T   T   T

Toni talked for an hour.

Toni talked for an hour.

Students trace and write the letter **T** and the sentence **Toni talked for an hour.**

Jane Jones

jeep

$\mathcal{J}$

$\mathcal{J}$ $\mathcal{J}$ $\mathcal{J}$ $\mathcal{J}$

Jane drives safely.

Jane drives safely.

Students trace and write the letter **J** and the sentence **Jane drives safely.**

U

Uncle Ulrich

usher

U U U   U

Uncle Ulrich saw a show.

Uncle Ulrich saw a show.

Students trace and write the letter **U** and the sentence **Uncle Ulrich saw a show.**

hill

Homer Hare

Homer got very cold.

Homer got very cold.

Students trace and write the letter **H** and the sentence **Homer got very cold.**

K

Kevin Kimball

kite

K K K K

Kevin makes his kite.

Kevin makes his kite.

Students trace and write the letter **K** and the sentence **Kevin makes his kite.**

Practice

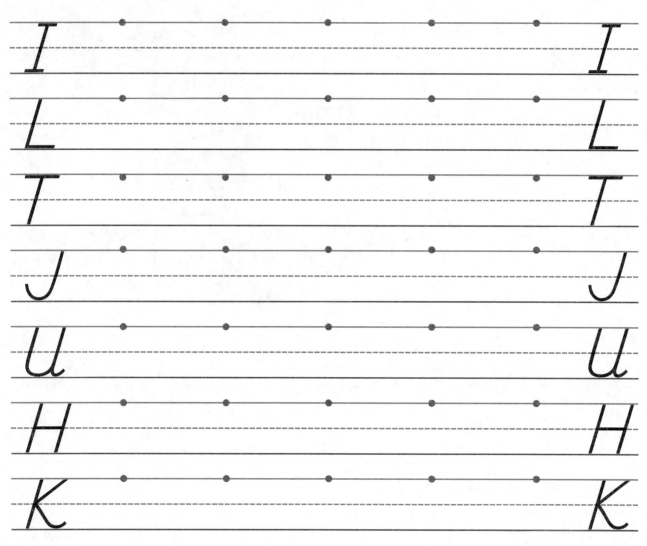

I   I

L   L

T   T

J   J

U   U

H   H

K   K

Circle your best letter in each line.

Students write the letters **I**, **L**, **T**, **J**, **U**, **H**, and **K**.

Review

Isabel

Isabel

Lucy

Lucy

Toni

Toni

Jane

Jane

Homer

Homer

Kevin

Kevin

Uncle Ulrich

Uncle Ulrich

Students trace and write names with the letters **I**, **L**, **T**, **J**, **U**, **H**, and **K**.

Evaluation

Remember: The letters **I** and **T** have crossbars.

Juri gave Irene a ride.

Juri gave Irene a ride.

They invited Kalel.

They invited Kalel.

Check Your Handwriting

Did you remember the crossbars for **I** and **T**?

Yes ☐   No ☐

Students trace and write sentences with the letters **I**, **T**, **J**, and **K**.

Anna Alpaca

Anna will be better.

Anna will be better.

Students trace and write the letter **A** and the sentence **Anna will be better.**

balloon

B

Becky Belle

B *B* *B* *B*

Becky lost her balloon.

Becky lost her balloon.

112 Writing **B**

Students trace and write the letter **B** and the sentence **Becky lost her balloon.**

Don Diaz

dinosaur

D

$D \quad D \quad D \quad D$

Don digs a big hole.

Don digs a big hole.

Students trace and write the letter **D** and the sentence **Don digs a big hole.**

mail

Mary
Moore

M M M M   M

Mary does a good job.

Mary does a good job.

114   Writing **M**

Students trace and write the letter **M** and the sentence **Mary does a good job.**

Nicky Norton

newspaper

N

N N N N

Nicky read for a while.

Nicky read for a while.

Students trace and write the letter **N** and the sentence **Nicky read for a while.**

picture

Paula Panda

P

P P P · · · P

Paula painted well.

Paula painted well.

Students trace and write the letter **P** and the sentence **Paula painted well.**

Rosie Rhino

R

rocket

R R R R   R

Rosie zoomed away.

Rosie zoomed away.

Students trace and write the letter **R** and the sentence **Rosie zoomed away.**

Practice

A   A

B   B

D   D

M   M

N   N

P   P

R   R

Circle your best letter in each line.

118 Practice

Students write the letters **A**, **B**, **D**, **M**, **N**, **P**, and **R**.

Review

Anna

Anna

Don

Don

Becky

Becky

Mary

Mary

Nicky

Nicky

Paula

Paula

Rosie Rhino

Rosie Rhino

Students trace and write names with the
letters **A**, **B**, **D**, **M**, **N**, **P**, and **R**.

Evaluation

Remember: Close the letters **D**, **P**, and **R**.

Does Pamela have paints?

Does Pamela have paints?

Aisha and Ramla smile.

Aisha and Ramla smile.

Check Your Handwriting

Did your close the letters **D**, **P**, and **R**?

Yes ☐   No ☐

Students trace and write sentences with the letters **A**, **D**, **P**, and **R**.

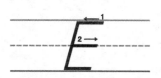

engine

Eddie Elf

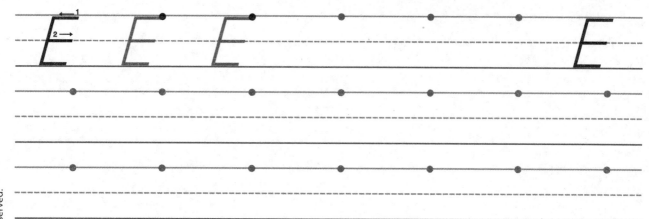

Eddie liked to ride.

Eddie liked to ride.

Students trace and write the letter **E** and the sentence **Eddie liked to ride.**

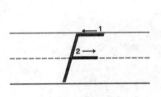

farm

Fay Fine

F F F F

Fay gets up early.

Fay gets up early.

122 Writing **F**

Students trace and write the letter **F** and the sentence **Fay gets up early.**

Z

Zack Zole

zipper

Z Z Z Z Z

Zack fixed his jacket.

Zack fixed his jacket.

Students trace and write the letter **Z** and the sentence **Zack fixed his jacket.**

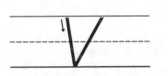

violin

Vi Vega

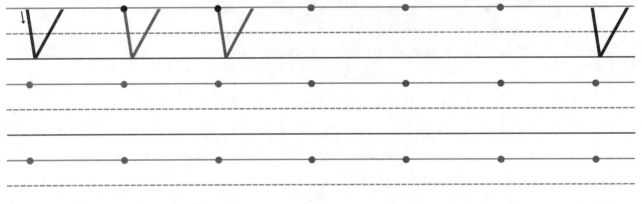

Vi plays nice tunes.

Vi plays nice tunes.

Students trace and write the letter **V** and the sentence **Vi plays nice tunes.**

window

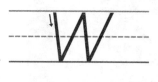

Walt Woodchuck

W W W W   W

Walt looks outside.

Walt looks outside.

Students trace and write the letter **W** and the sentence **Walt looks outside.**

Mr. Xter

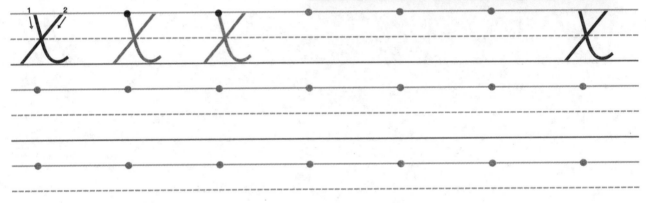

Mr. Xter is an acrobat.

Mr. Xter is an acrobat.

Students trace and write the letter **X** and the sentence **Mr. Xter is an acrobat.**

Yelda Yak

yams

Y Y Y Y

Yelda eats her treats.

Yelda eats her treats.

Students trace and write the letter **Y** and the sentence **Yelda eats her treats.**

Practice

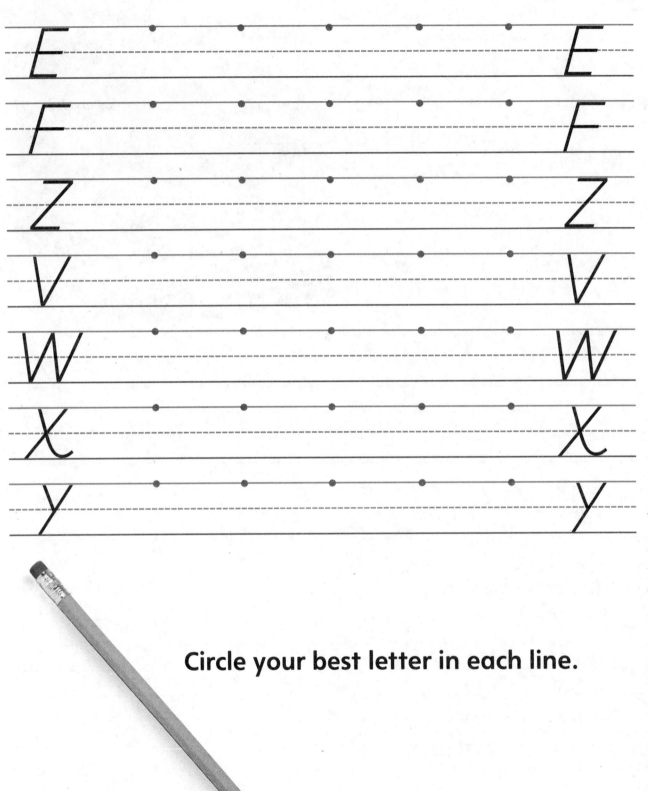

E   E

F   F

Z   Z

V   V

W   W

X   X

Y   Y

Circle your best letter in each line.

Students write the letters **E**, **F**, **Z**, **V**, **W**, **X**, and **Y**.

Review

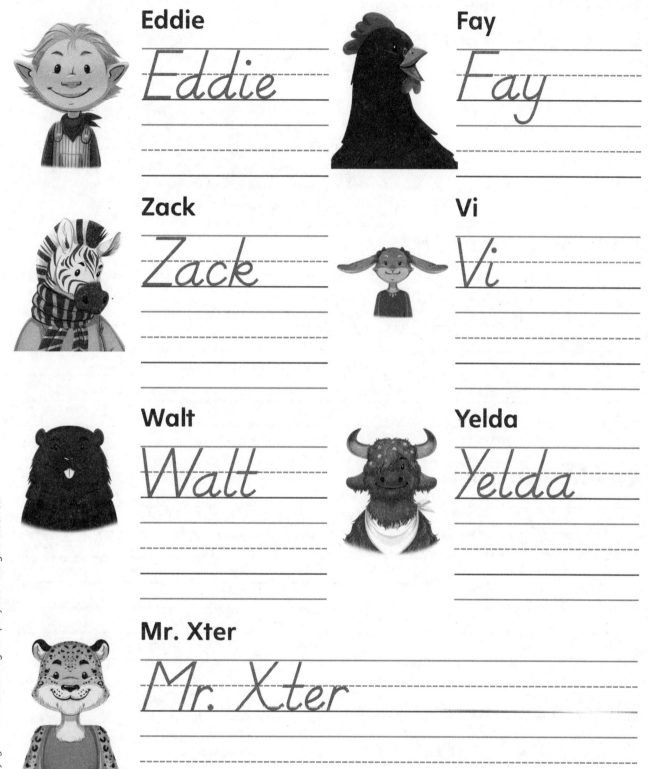

Eddie

Eddie

Fay

Fay

Zack

Zack

Vi

Vi

Walt

Walt

Yelda

Yelda

Mr. Xter

Mr. Xter

Students trace and write names with the letters **E, F, Z, V, W, X,** and **Y.**

Evaluation

Remember: Slant all the letters the same way.

Frida and Vera sing.

Frida and Vera sing.

Will Mr. Xter act?

Will Mr. Xter act?

Check Your Handwriting

	Yes	No
Do all your letters slant the same way?	☐	☐

Students trace and write sentences with the letters **F**, **V**, **W**, and **X**.

A   B   C   D

E   F   G   H

I   J   K   L

M   N   O   P

Q   R   S   T

U   V   W   X

Y   Z

Cumulative Review   **131**

Students write each capital letter of the alphabet.

You need to fill out a form for a library card.
Complete the form.

Library Card

Name _____

Address _____

City _____

You may need to fill out a form for a bus pass.
Complete the form.

BUS PASS

Name _____

School _____

Students complete forms for a library card and a bus pass.

There are seven days in a week.
Read the names in the correct order.

1. Sunday   2. Monday   3. Tuesday

4. Wednesday   5. Thursday   6. Friday   7. Saturday

Trace and write the names.

Sunday

Monday

Tuesday

Wednesday

Students trace and write the first four days of the week.

Thursday

Friday

Saturday

Pick your favorite day of the week.
What do you like to do?
Draw a picture.

134 Writing Days of the Week

Students trace and write the last three days of the week. Then
they draw a picture of their favorite activity for a specific day.

There are twelve months in the year.
Read the names in the correct order.

January

February

March

April

May

June

July

August

September

October

November

December

Trace and write the months.

January

February

March

April

Students trace and write the names of the first four months of the year.

May

June

July

August

September

October

November

December

136 Writing Months of the Year

Students trace and write the names of the last eight months of the year.

Sonia invited Laura to a party.
Read Sonia's invitation.

To: *Laura*

What: *Sleepover Party*

When: *Friday at 6:00 P.M.*

Where: *27 Long Street*

From: *Sonia*

Copy the invitation on your own paper.
Don't forget to close the letters **a**, **d**, **o**, and **g**.

Writing an Invitation   **137**

Students copy an invitation.

Laura wrote to Sonia to thank her for her party.
Read Laura's thank-you note.

April 24, 202_

Dear Sonia,

Your sleepover party
was fun. Thank you.

Your pal,

Laura

Copy the thank-you note on your own paper.
Remember to slant your letters the same way.

Students copy a thank-you note.

Read the directions for making a bookmark.

1. Get paper and crayons.

2. Draw a pet you like.

3. Write your name on the bookmark.

4. Cut it out carefully.

5. Put it inside a book.

Copy the directions on your own paper.

Leave more space between words than between letters.

Now follow the directions. Make a bookmark.

Students copy a set of directions for making a bookmark.
Then they use the directions to make their own bookmark.

Read the joke. Then copy it.
Remember to use capital letters.
Don't forget to use these marks.

| ? | . | ' | , |

Jim, where's your dog?

I don't know.

Do you give up?

Yes, I do.

It's in a barking lot.

Students copy a joke without a handwriting model.

Writing a Math Test

Good handwriting helps you do well on math tests.

Good handwriting makes your numbers and words easy to read.

Getting Ready

- Read the test question carefully.

- Be sure you understand what the question is asking you to do.

Finding a Pattern

What comes next in the pattern?

Look at the numbers and shapes.

See how they repeat to make a pattern.

- Use your best handwriting.
  All your numbers should slant the same way.

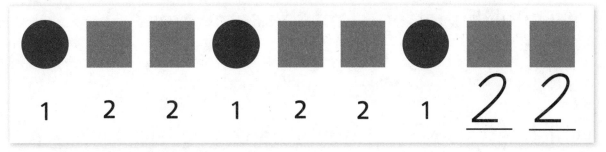

- If you make a mistake, fix it as your teacher tells you.
  Which should you do?
  Draw a line through it and rewrite it. ☐
  Erase it carefully and rewrite it. ☐

Students identify and extend number and letter patterns and evaluate their own handwriting.

Paul completed the letter pattern below.
Then he wrote what the pattern is.

What letters complete the pattern? Tell what the
pattern is.

b　c　c　b　c　c　b　_cc_　_b_

The ~~patern~~ is bcc.   pattern

Look at Paul's answer.　　　　　　　Yes　　No

- Did he write only one letter on
  each answer line?
- Do all his letters slant the same way?
- Is his handwriting easy to read?
- Did he fix mistakes carefully?

Which letters do not have the correct slant?
Circle them.

Cross out Paul's incorrect answers.
Write the correct letter over each answer line.

Now you find the missing numbers in the pattern below.
Write what the pattern is.

What numbers complete the pattern? Tell what the pattern is.

■	▲	▲	■	▲	▲	■	▲	▲
7	8	8	7	8	8	7	___	___

_____

_____

_____

_____

_____

_____

Check your handwriting.

Yes   No

- Did you write only one number on each answer line?
- Do all your numbers slant the same way?
- Is your handwriting easy to read?
- Did you fix mistakes carefully?

Circle the word in your answer that shows your best writing.